REACH for the Visionary Woman of God

With the Father, Son, and Holy Spirit I Can Do All Things

Avis Winifred

WestBow
PRESS

WestBow Press books may be ordered through booksellers or by contacting:

WestBow Press
A Division of Thomas Nelson
1663 Liberty Drive
Bloomington, IN 47403
www.westbowpress.com
1-(866) 928-1240

Because of the dynamic nature of the Internet, any Web addresses or links contained in this book may have changed since publication and may no longer be valid. The views expressed in this work are solely those of the author and do not necessarily reflect the views of the publisher, and the publisher hereby disclaims any responsibility for them.

ISBN: 978-1-4497-0342-4 (sc)
ISBN: 978-1-4497-0343-1 (e)

Library of Congress Control Number: 2010933028

Printed in the United States of America

WestBow Press rev. date:10/26/2010

Contents

Words of Wisdom

I can do all things through Christ who
strengthens me.
Philippians 4:13

Dear Readers,

I think it's important for you to know a little about your author.

If we are truly spiritual women, we rely on more than our natural instincts and intellectual faculties to determine if we are receiving solid instruction. With this said—get to know me for a second.

While you are reading this letter (and the entire book for that matter), couple your investigation with prayer.

My name is Avis Winifred. My father, the late Morris Anderson, Jr., named me and all my other siblings; however, it was not until my late 30s that I discovered the spiritual meaning of my name.

During a Bible study at a church in Corpus Christi, TX, the facilitator of the session informed me that my name meant "mighty in the Spirit." This was very refreshing, and its value was reinforced when I took my first evangelism trip to Africa. Upon leaving the airport, my host passed through a small town named *Avis*. I can assure you, at that moment I knew I was in the right place at the right time.

I believe my Christian walk, although not perfect, has been shaped by my yielding to the Spirit of God and by my desire to fulfill the purposes God has intended for my life.

My sustaining motto has always been "I do not want to leave this world failing to accomplish everything God has purposed for my life." With this kind of tenacity, my favorite verse since the age of 11 is most fitting: I must work the works of Him who sent Me while it is day; *the* night is coming when no one can work (John 9:4).

I am a single mother of a *grown* son (24 as this book goes to print). He has been my friend, prayer partner, and Bible study partner, and I've even raised him to confront gently spiritual discrepancies he may note in my life—trust me, this works both ways.

My long gone grandmother, Mary Frances, and my mother, Florence Louise, modeled what it meant to have a personal relationship with God and to rely on the guidance of the Holy Spirit.

The woman God created me to be has helped sustain that modeled relationship and to dismantle, or at least disrupt, situations created to hinder my union with the Trinity.

I am an advocate of education—thus, degrees in business, composition, rhetoric and writing and postgraduate study in theology decorate my office walls and sustain my critical and spiritual approach to life.

With this background, you can expect that my ministry in writing requires audience members not merely to passively observe, but to engage their minds, hearts, and spirits for the purpose of change.

My parents raised me with a firm work ethic, so slothfulness and absenteeism have not been a part of my professional or educational life. Consequently, it took a six-week medical leave of absence from my job for God to birth this book while I was homebound recovering from surgery.

My professional life has resided in two arenas, management and teaching at the college level. The latter profession has taken me to Italy four times, Africa twice, Spain, and Ireland—so far. While I've also walked the soils of Mexico, Montreal, and British Columbia, I'm hopeful that my next career move will take me all over the world, bringing words of peace and hope to hurting people, communities, corporations, governments, and ministries.

I know from personal experience that we have to take time to stop and listen to God. I also know that if we don't do it, God will arrange that time for us because He loves us just that much.

Finally, I believe that if God took the time to give me this word in *REACH*, it may reward you richly to approach its content with openness, honesty, and above all prayer to see how it is intended for your life.

And, I must add, I hope you approach the book with the goal of change and transformation—addressing those issues that may have compromised vision living. Thus, complete all the noted written sections so that you begin to take ownership of the book's content.

Sisters, I love you. I will never be jealous of you. I want you to do, have, and give all that God intended in your purposeful lives.

Your Sister in Christ,
Avis Winifred, Ph. D.

Words of Wisdom

But this *I say:* He who sows sparingly will
also reap sparingly, and he who sows bountifully
will also reap bountifully.
2 Corinthians 9:6

Frances A Woman of REACH in Action

One November morning around 4:00 a.m., Frances awoke to begin her devotion. She propped herself in her bed and placed the needed materials neatly around her left and right side—a cleansing prayer, her Bible, a current *Upper Room* devotional booklet, a wisdom book, and her journal.

Midway through her time with God, Frances stopped. She said, "Lord, I'm ready. I am ready to be that storm you intended me to be."

As Frances slept alone every night, she could have shouted those words, but she didn't. She whispered them to God; she whispered because she was surprised by the confession she had just made, yet she was in complete peace.

For the average person, a storm is a troubling time in life—moments filled with struggle and pain. But that's not what Frances envisioned. Frances saw her life, her gift, as a huge rolling cloud just waiting to burst forth the nourishing waters that would release potential in so many corners of the world.

Frances was willing to yield to a vision God had placed in her spirit—as unthinkable as that was for this young woman. At that moment of yielding, she turned from complacency to faithfulness.

Early that November morning Frances chose to yield to God; she desired to be a Woman of *REACH*.

Look in the Mirror—How are you similar or different?

Words of Wisdom

Wisdom and knowledge will be the stability
of your times,
And the strength of salvation;
The fear of the LORD *is* His treasure.
Isaiah 33:6

Biblical Women Who Exhibit REACH Qualities

Using your Bible, look up the passages noted below that share complete or partial glimpses into the lives of these women. After reading the scriptures, record the qualities you most appreciate. *(See Appendix C for my responses)*

Abigail
Read: I Samuel 25:1-42
Qualities you admire in Abigail:

Esther
Read: Esther 3:1-4:17
Qualities you admire in Esther:

Hannah
Read: I Samuel 1:20
Qualities you admire in Hannah:

Lydia
Read: Acts 16:11-40
Qualities you admire in Lydia:

Mary, the Mother of Jesus
Read: Luke 1:26-38
Qualities you admire in Mary, the Mother of Jesus:

Tabitha
Read: Acts 9:36-42
Qualities you admire in Tabitha:

The Woman with an Issue of Blood
Read: Luke 8:40-48
Qualities you admire in The Woman with an Issue of Blood:

The Proverbs 31 Woman
Read: Proverbs 31:10-31
Qualities you admire in The Proverbs 31 Woman:

Ruth
Read: Ruth 1:16-17
Qualities you admire in Ruth:

Glean the Most from REACH

Take Your Time

What happens if you walk into a movie theater and you are thirty minutes late for the film, or you begin on page fifteen of a fifty-page book? The answer is that you miss something valuable. You miss the beginning that establishes the foundation for what you are about to view or read. So, take your time with *REACH for the Visionary Woman of God*. Don't just skim through or complete a quick read without also completing the requested written responses.

I am a reader of Christian inspirational literature, and a number of books have resided on my shelf—untouched—for months or even years at a time. However, it has never failed that when the time was right, when my heart was ready to receive and my ears truly positioned for listening, I removed those books from their respective resting places and seized the words of encouragement and the guidance needed during those perfect times of instruction. I read these sources of inspiration from cover to cover. Skipping a page or two meant I could miss out on the very word, phrase, or example I was in need of.

Furthermore, having become more sensitive to timely instruction in the last couple of years, I have begun to ask the Spirit to guide my understanding as I approach new words of wisdom, and to open my heart to receive what I need from God's gifted writers.

It has been during these honest pleas for guidance in understanding that I have begun to more appropriately apply the principles of instruction God intended for me in the thousands and thousands of precious words between the book covers of inspirational writers. If we are submissive, good books and good teachers have a lot to offer us now and for the rest of our lives.

With these words, I urge you to take your time in reading REACH and to invest serious thought and action in applying the content to your life. To merely read the book and say "that was an interesting read" will do little for supporting your God-vision. Position yourself to hear, receive, and act on the instruction in these pages.

Understand the Key Principles

There are distinguishing principles that guide a woman of REACH. Several of these may be foundational to your thinking. Others may need to be strengthened through prayer and commitment.

Principle #1

A Woman of REACH welcomes the opportunity to move to new levels in her bond with Christ, knowing fully that growing pains and trying situations are a part of the journey.

Principle #2

A Woman of REACH is honest with herself and with God. She understands that lying defeats potential and growth, and it surely works against the healing and guiding hands of God.

Principle #3

A Woman of REACH, in the midst of it all, confesses that she is not superwoman, but she is willing and prudent enough to release what God has already placed within—gifts, purpose, and joy—knowing that the Holy Spirit will lead her into continual growth if she does so. In God's light, she is amazing.

Principle #4

A Woman of REACH pursues an approach, a way of life, an attitude that she nourishes while in a committed relationship with God.

Principle #5

A Woman of REACH is observant and cautious—in other words, she's no fool. She listens and watches for those who are jealous, biased, angry, frustrated, fearful, and even lazy. The ones presenting such traits may be unbelievers or believers who, for a moment in time, gave up and in their despair lashed out at the Woman of REACH.

Likewise, the Woman of REACH monitors her own attitude and behavior. She realizes that if she takes her eyes and mind off the source of all that she is, even for a moment, she too could become puffed up and a distraction to herself and to others.

Confront the Challenges

Principles are wonderful; they guide our daily living. However, sometimes we may be willing to compromise our principles because of something that appears to be more pressing. For example, you may need to ask yourself the following questions:

> What *appears* to be stopping me from being the one whom God has called me to be?

> What *appears* to be blocking me from doing what God has called me to do?

> What *appears* to be getting in the way of my God-given vision that's burning in my spirit?

As you contemplate the above questions, could the answers fall into one or several of these areas?

- A past that's complicating the present and/or the future
- A present that shows no significant change or serious effort to support a better future
- A future that's never been envisioned or one that's been denied or rejected

Notice, I've stressed the word "appears" because God's children are going to face challenges, but we can turn situations around if we approach them with God. What you think is a challenge could be the most effective learning, growing, strengthening, or developing moment in your life—if you let God intervene or speak to you about your past, present, and future—Principle #1:

A Woman of REACH welcomes the opportunity to move to new levels in her bond with Christ, knowing fully that growing pains and trying situations are a part of the journey.

Yolanda A Woman of REACH in Action

Yolanda has been a believer for many years, but only in the last few months has she truly begun to surrender every aspect of her life to God. She realized she was living a compromised spiritual life, that is, a life that was in jeopardy of not receiving all the peace and blessings that accompany a life of surrender.

Her focused, Spirit-filled journey began when she asked God for wisdom, knowledge, discernment, and understanding in every aspect of her life. And when she coupled this request with a commitment to be truthful, her life began to transform. In this season of honesty, Yolanda admitted that previously she had chosen to give God only restricted access to her life. There were personal, professional, and even spiritual arenas Yolanda had closed from God's reign.

When the camouflaged surrender to God ceased, when the lies ceased, and when confession was coupled with God's grace and forgiveness, Yolanda discovered

- she was holding on to a past that kept her in bondage;
- she had been keeping company with people who were being used by Satan to plant seeds of doubt and nurture past fears, and who attempted to compromise Yolanda's future because they had no vision of their own.

By opening her spiritual eyes, Yolanda began to see that she had been concurring with these negative thoughts and thus had been sabotaging her potential to do great things for God's people and to fulfill the potential God had placed in her life. Yolanda realized that she no longer had to follow a pattern that accepted a mediocrity nourished by her unaddressed fears, which ultimately led to slothfulness and anxiety.

Once Yolanda became aware of the deception planted by her own mind by Satan and by the people who allowed themselves to be instruments of that which works against God, Yolanda began to trace her shortcomings as a believer to many unhealed areas in her past, areas she had not released to God.

What Yolanda was really discovering was that she had not trusted God to shape and secure her life, her gifts, her potential, her call. However, in a confession that said "no more compromise," Yolanda allowed submission to God, commitment to the Word of God, and an invitation for healing to birth a life aimed at liberation. This brought freedom from ignorance and from every fruit associated with deception.

Women of REACH choose to see and respond with spiritual eyes. They realize nothing can or should be concealed from God.

Look in the Mirror—How are you similar or different?

Words of Wisdom

But whoever listens to me will dwell safely,
And will be secure, without fear of evil."
Proverbs 1:33

For we do not wrestle against flesh and blood,
but against principalities, against powers,
against the rulers of the darkness of this age,
against spiritual *hosts* of wickedness in the
heavenly *places.* Therefore take up the whole
armor of God, that you may be able to withstand
in the evil day, and having done all, to
stand.
Ephesians 6:12-13

For though we walk in the flesh, we do not
war according to the flesh. For the weapons
of our warfare *are* not carnal but mighty in
God for pulling down strongholds, casting
down arguments and every high thing that
exalts itself against the knowledge of God,
bringing every thought into captivity to the
obedience of Christ.
2 Corinthians 10:3-5

Look in the Mirror

On several occasions when I have facilitated seminars, I have strategically placed mirrors around the room or even placed them in attendees' packets. When we have reached a critical moment in the presentation, I've asked my audience members to pull out those mirrors and to confront what they see while I ask investigative questions.

Once everyone gets beyond the physical blemishes, the hair out of place, or whatever seems to be displeasing, I call us all back to the issue at hand. Those first reactions are simply distractions or avoidance tactics—we all have them.

In this book, I'm going to ask you to look in the mirror. In some instances, you'll answer a series of questions, and in other cases you'll compare the behaviors of a Woman of REACH to your own behaviors. This is exactly what Yolanda did, and you see how it began to turn her life around. In the *Look in the Mirror* reflections, always be honest—Principle #2:

A Woman of REACH is honest with herself and with God. She understands that lying defeats potential and growth, and it surely works against the healing and guiding hands of God.

Go back to the vignettes about Frances and Yolanda to determine if you need to make a few revisions to your earlier *Look in the Mirror* reflections.

Examine Your Circle of Influence

As you consider the basic principles for a Woman of REACH, you need to engage in a little inventory. Take time to reflect on how central God has been in your life. Such an exploration may determine what or who has formed the principles by which you live and how you have chosen to respond to the life God has given you.

#1 When did you accept Jesus Christ as your Savior?

#2 When did you begin to surrender (a) your finances, (b) your family, (c) your love life, (d) your professional life, (e) your health, and (f) your dreams to God?

Briefly note events that show each area of surrender. Leave blank those areas you have not yet surrendered.

a.

b.

c.

d.

e.

f.

#3 Review the above. What's holding you back from releasing certain areas in your life? Be honest!

#4 Do you feel that your spiritual life is being compromised in any way? Think about friends, activities, thoughts, events and people from the past or the present. List any that seem applicable.

#5 Is there something in your past, your present, or your future that's holding you captive? Are you afraid to move forward in some area of your life?

Make a list of these.

#6 Are there people in your life planting negative thoughts in your mind, and thus blocking the view of a satisfying and fruitful present or future? Name these people.

#7 Is there any way in which you see yourself as mediocre because of some activity, some past event, some words spoken about your life? Write out your concerns.

#8 Looking at your response to #7, do you think God would agree? Why or why not?

Prayer Time

Go back over your responses to questions 1-8. As you review each one, ask God to forgive you in those areas where you have not trusted Him. Next, ask God to guide you out of unhealthy relationships or to heal those that you should maintain. Third, ask God to lead you in a spiritual life that shouts "no more compromises."

In this prayer, honestly tell God that you are willing to release every aspect of your existence that is not in line with the Spirit-filled life He intends you to live.

And finally, ask God to create a hunger for His Word that nourishes and guides the holy and obedient life you desire to live and that He wants you to live.

Compose a prayer that reflects these requests and then date the prayer. As we are all human, you may find the need to return to this prayer from time to time.

Lord,

Date _____

If you have been honest with the above, you are well on your way to becoming a Woman of REACH who chooses to see and respond with spiritual eyes.

Words of Wisdom

Test all things; hold fast what is good.
1 Thessalonians 5:21

Words of Wisdom

Delight yourself also in the LORD,
And He shall give you the desires of your
heart.
Psalm 37:4

RISE TO YOUR POTENTIAL
THROUGH GOD

Vicky A Woman of REACH in Action

Vicky is 40-years-old. She suffers from lower back pain on occasion, and she weighs about 285 pounds.

Now, what if Vicky confessed that she wanted to become a ballerina? What would you say, and, if not out loud, what would you think?

Pause . . . .

The real issue is not what you think about Vicky. What matters is what Vicky believes about herself, her potential, and the source of her strength.

All outsiders can see is Vicky's size, what's visible to the eye. What the onlookers don't know is that the day Vicky made that confession, she began altering her eating habits. She started swimming and walking and made a commitment for these activities to be a part of her weekly routine. She's committed to living a healthy life that will manifest itself in a smaller and healthier body.

It isn't that Vicky truthfully sees herself as a ballerina. The vision is a metaphor for what she really wants. Vicky wants to offer herself as an attractive, healthy, and vibrant gift to her future husband.

She has realized that a lack of discipline has sabotaged her outer portrait as well as seeped into spiritual areas of her life.

Vicky wants not only her outside to be appealing to her partner, but her inner spirit as well.

Vicky believes her husband will be a gift from God, her co-partner in the ministry. Consequently, she wants to present herself as a treasured gift, beautifully and distinctively appealing to the mate God will bring to her.

Women of REACH are not dependent on the confirmation of others, but rather on the One who dwells within.

Look in the Mirror—How are you similar or different?

Words of Wisdom

Do you not know that you are the temple
of God and *that* the Spirit of God dwells in
you?
1 Corinthians 3:16

The Metaphor

You know a picture can irrupt thousands of thoughts. You also know that if you can visualize something in your mind, you can come to terms with the subject just a little better.

I will go a step further. If you can wrap your mind around a vision, pull all the intricate pieces together, you are in a better position to live out the steps to achieve that vision.

The next several pages will introduce the motivating image for a Woman of REACH—the gifted ballerina. If you have seen a poised and balanced ballerina dance, then you have seen the metaphor for what I call the Woman of REACH.

Now, you may be saying, I have nothing in common with a ballerina. I don't dance, I don't have the body for it, I'm past the years of ever standing on my toes, or _____ (Fill in your reservation.).

If any of those thoughts came to your mind as you read the word "ballerina," then you have specifically addressed the very reason why I selected the ballerina as the metaphor.

A Woman of REACH does what God says she can do, not what others think or even what she may at times perceive she's capable of.

When a called woman of God is operating in God's glory and for God's glory, she is as amazing, as graceful, and as beautiful as an angelic ballerina—Principle #3:

A Woman of REACH, in the midst of it all, confesses that she is not superwoman, but she is willing and prudent enough to release what God has already placed within—gifts, purpose, and joy—knowing that the Holy Spirit will lead her into continual growth if she does so. In God's light, she is amazing.

A Visionary

Picture this angelic ballerina. She is elegant and poised. Her stance makes onlookers believe that she was born for excellence; she appears naturally gifted.

However, a good dancer does not acquire the ability to take her graceful positions overnight. It takes hard work, continual practice, and a firm belief that she can dance, and dance well.

In fact, there is that one climatic position for the ballerina that clearly shouts, "I have arrived. I have REACHed my destiny!"

Keep in mind, however, the ballerina does not stay in her climatic position continuously. It is timed and executed at the right moment.

For that timely executed position, the angelic ballerina has to prepare herself to extend beyond the norm while maintaining balance—that's what visionary people do.

Words of Wisdom

I press toward the goal for the prize of the
upward call of God in Christ Jesus.
Philippians 3:14

God's Ballerina

A Woman of REACH does those things that please and honor her Lord and Savior.

She's talented, gifted, and equipped; however, acknowledgement of Him to whom she belongs, and thus

> the character she has inherited living as a child of the King,
> an acceptance of her gift given by God, and
> insightful preparation (through the Spirit)

are the resources that will aid in her destiny—the peak of her God-given moments.

God has chosen you. He desires you to walk the journey as you aim to live out the vision He's planted in your spirit. Rising to your potential is not a choice—it's a calling.

Words of Wisdom

"I am the vine, you *are* the branches. He who abides in Me, and I in Him, bears much fruit; for without Me you can do nothing. If anyone does not abide in Me, he is cast out as a branch and is withered; and they gather them and throw *them* into the fire, and they are burned. If you abide in Me, and My words abide in you, you will ask what you desire, and it shall be done for you. By this My Father is glorified, that you bear much fruit; so you will be My disciples.
John 15:5-8

Let us hold fast the confession of *our* hope without wavering, for He who promised *is* faithful.
Hebrews 10:23

Diane A Woman of REACH in Action

Diane is 24-years-old. She's about to graduate from law school. For years she's talked about becoming a lawyer, but ever since she began attending the small church in her college town, she's felt a call to move in an altered direction: the missionary field and then legal counsel for non-profit organizations supporting third-world countries.

Diane's mother, however, holds the view of her daughter the *corporate lawyer* on a pedestal. And Diane has not come up with the courage to share the revised vision for her life. She does not want to disappoint her mother.

What's sad is that her mom senses something different about Diane and fears she may be moving away from what *they* had planned for Diane's life, so her mom reiterates, every chance she gets, what a wonderful contribution Diane will be to a multimillion-dollar company.

After praying and fasting, Diane realizes what's taking place and has a long chat with her mother. The subject is "God's presence in each believer's life, to protect, guide, and instruct."

Women of REACH seek out and discern God's voice and then respond to His voice.

Look in the Mirror—How are you similar or different?

Clarifying the Image: Distinguishing Features of a Woman of REACH

Who?

> REACH is practiced by a woman who is completely committed to Jesus and to the things that concern God. Selfishness has no place in her way of life. A Woman of REACH realizes who she is in Christ and the gift she will be to the world.

What?

> Being successful through God, with God, and in God. This is your state of being.

Why?

> To fulfill the things God's planted in your heart and to help others in the process is a vital mission.Birth the potential within. Remember, if God's intended it for you, it's going to impact others. We live in communities, so do not deny others.

When?

> Consistent preparation without extensive periods of down time is the norm.

Where?

> In every arena of your life. Give God full access—personal, professional, educational, etc.

How?

> *Boldly*—dare to see God's destiny.

Fearlessly—arm to move with hope.

Relentlessly—determine not to give up.

Courageously—walk like the Trinity is behind every move.

Submissively—seize the strength by releasing all into God's hands.

Diligently—flee from laziness.

Sacrificially—realize the difference between planting and harvesting.

Joyously—celebrate the journey.

Perseveringly—push ahead in spite of the challenges.

Faithfully—remember all things work together for the good of those that love the Lord and who are called for His purposes.

Creatively—choose to be flexible in the pursuit.

Principle #4:

A Woman of REACH pursues an approach, a way of life, an attitude that she nourishes while in a committed relationship with God.

Words of Wisdom

Therefore, if anyone *is* in Christ, *he is* a
new creation; old things have passed away;
behold, all things have become new.
2 Corinthians 5:17

Karen, Karla, Rhonda and Joyce Women of REACH in Action

One fall, Dr. Johnson was invited to be a guest speaker in a city about four hours away from her home. She accepted the invitation and spent hours preparing for the presentation.

Since she wanted things to go well, Dr. Johnson drove down early and spent an afternoon speaking with the young inner city girls who would comprise her audience.

She spent some time before her presentation getting to know a few of the young women. Among the group were up-and-coming intellectuals like Karen, entertainers like Karla, humanitarians like Rhonda, care providers like Joyce.

After a few hours with these young women, Dr. Johnson changed her introduction to address these amazing 14-18-year-olds.

While this was not a Christian speaking engagement, certain Christian principles—believe in yourself, aim high, and trust that if you try and assist others along the way, many will be blessed—were still appropriate.

The next afternoon, before a crowd of almost 200 people, Dr. Johnson began with the following:

Greetings!
Future Presidents, Computer Scientists,
Global Accountants, Professors, Lawyers,
Doctors, CEOs, Class Presidents, Chaplains,
Prime Ministers, Valedictorians and
Salutatorians, Teachers, Track Stars, Nurses,
Vocalists, Managers, World Travelers, & _____

Yes, these titles are correct, young women, because each one of you is capable of achieving the seemingly impossible that will impact your life and the lives of those around you.

Women of REACH begin to live out their own potential before they are really aware of what they are doing. The calling becomes a part of their everyday world; consequently, they alert others to their potential.

Look in the Mirror—How are you similar or different?

Words of Wisdom

Commit your works to the Lord, and your
thoughts will be established.
Proverbs 16:3

EXCEL IN THE WORD OF GOD FOR CLEAR DIRECTION

Setting the Stage for Vision Living: Hunger for the Word

There's no substitute for God's Word. Neither the best written book nor the most insightful sermon nor the piercing power of a song compare to what God will speak into your spirit as you pour yourself into His Word.

Committed reading, pondering, accepting, and praying over God's Word will revolutionize your thinking, your living, your walking—your very being.

Remember, though, in a chaotic world where you are pressed for time, where many voices spill into your thinking, and where the things of God seem contrary to what's popular, you must be determined to stay in the Word.

Give God's Word your undivided attention and see what He will speak into your spirit.

Tip: If it's a challenge to get started, ask God to create a desperate hunger in you for His Word and His presence in your life—see what will come from such a request.

Words of Wisdom

Be diligent to present yourself approved
to God, a worker who does not need to be
ashamed, rightly dividing the word of truth.
2 Timothy 2:15

I will instruct you and teach you in the way
you should go;
I will guide you with My eye.
Psalm 32:8

Take firm hold of instruction, do not let go;
Keep her, for she *is* your life.
Proverbs 4:13

And you will seek Me and find *Me,* when you
search for Me with all your heart.
Jeremiah 29:13

For the word of God *is* living and powerful,
and sharper than any two-edged sword,
piercing even to the division of soul and spirit,
and of joints and marrow, and is a discerner
of the thoughts and intents of the heart.
Hebrews 4:12

Visions

Women of REACH choose to have a vision, a dream for their lives. Women committed to living the Word of God *can't help but have* a vision for their lives because God is present, active, and breathing hope into their very existence.

Consequently, having a vision is a part of being a believer, for a vision embraces a productive and fulfilled future that aims to serve God and provide a blessing for others.

Understand clearly, however, that such a vision is something that will take effort, hard work, and a commitment to seek God's counsel before, during, and after completion.

Finally, there is one other key component to visions—a complicated component that others often do not understand. Either they just can't see it or they refuse to acknowledge God's power in your life.

The solution here is to be mindful of where people are in their own walk with God when they attempt to counsel you about your God-given vision.

While taking these people's comments into consideration, ask God in prayer if they are really ready to embrace your vision—Principle #5.

A Woman of REACH at last is observant and cautious—In other words, she's no fool. She listens
and watches for those who are jealous, biased, angry, frustrated, fearful, and even lazy. The ones presenting such traits may be unbelievers or believers who for a moment in time gave up and in their despair lashed out at the Woman of REACH. Likewise, the Woman of REACH monitors her own attitude and behavior. She realizes that if she, if only for a moment, takes her eyes and mind off the source of all that she is, she too could become puffed up and a distraction.

Words of Wisdom

So we fasted and entreated our God for this,
and He answered our prayer.
Ezra 8:23

Create in me a clean heart, O God,
And renew a steadfast spirit within me.
Psalm 51:10

Search me, O God, and know my heart;
Try me, and know my anxieties; And see
if *there is any* wicked way in me,
And lead me in the way everlasting.
Psalm 139: 23-24

Not that I have already attained, or am already
perfected; but I press on, that I may lay hold
of that for which Christ Jesus has also laid
hold of me.
Philippians 3:12

Esther

Do you recall Esther, the orphaned child?

What do you think Esther's friends said when she told them she was going to prepare for the position of queen? There was no way they could have envisioned the plan God had in store for Esther, nor the doors that would be opened for her to save her people.

Do you recall what Esther and her servants did before Esther agreed to meet with the king at an ill-appointed time? They fasted and prayed.

God may have bigger plans for your life than you or those around you do; however, if you choose not to participate in God's plan, you'll never know the outcome.

I encourage you to reread (or read) the Book of Esther. As you examine her life, think about the following:

- Her background
- Her preparation that readied her for a new path
- Her influential counsel
- Her spiritual steps that guided wise movements
- Her ultimate achievement for her people

Ruth

Do you recall Ruth, the widow displaced from her birth family?

What do you think Ruth's mother and father desired for her when her husband died? Who wouldn't want their child to return home? There was no way they could have envisioned the plan God had in store for Ruth, nor the blessings her children and children's children would usher in for the people of God.

Do you recall what Ruth did before she encountered Boaz on the threshing floor? She sought seasoned counsel.

God may have bigger plans for your life than your mother and father do; however, if you choose not to participate in God's plan, you'll never know the outcome.

I encourage you to read (or re-read) the Book of Ruth. As you examine her life, think about the following:

- Her background
- Her preparation that readied her for a new path
- Her influential counsel
- Her spiritual steps (specifically her choice to honor the monotheistic God of Naomi) that guided wise movements
- Her ultimate achievement for the people of God

Words of Wisdom

. . . . Yet who knows whether you have come
to the kingdom for *such* a time as this?"
Esther 4:14

Look in the Mirror

#1 What do you see yourself achieving in your personal life—short term and/or long term?

#2 What do you see yourself doing in your professional life—short term and/or long term?

#3 What do you see yourself doing in your spiritual life—short term and/or long term?

Trace back the development of these visions.

Are they yours or are they God-inspired? A good way to distinguish between the two roots is to determine the fruits and who will benefit.

Are they all about you and yours, or do they support the people of God and God's kingdom?

Taking a Practical Approach

Choose one vision you feel is God-given. What practical activities do you see supporting this potential achievement? List the things you will have to do to live the vision. Consider training, academic classes, volunteer work, reading materials, organization membership, collaborations, mentoring, networking, etc. that will support your complete engagement in the vision.

Don't worry about the order just yet. This is a brainstorming activity that requires only a forecasting of ideas.

#1

#2

#3

#4

#5

#6

#8

#9

#10

Moving Like a Godly Woman: A Call from Heaven

There is one unique feature of the godly woman who participates in REACHing. Her dreams may not be typical of the angelic ballerina. They will certainly differ from those of the Christian woman who has *not* envisioned the endless possibilities inherent in serving and being a gift to others through God.

God's REACHing woman moves steadily towards the heavenly Father.

While the earthly ballerina must obey the choreographer's directions, the music's tempo, the ballet's story, the REACHing, angelic ballerina keeps her sights fixed only on God.

For the committed woman of God, her direction is always towards her heavenly Father, always aiming for what seems like that *almost* unreachable vision that God has planted in her spirit.

It is only when a woman of God moves in God's direction through faith, commitment, and attention to God's Word and love that God-given dreams come into existence.

Words of Wisdom

I press toward the goal for the prize of the
upward call of God in Christ Jesus.
Philippians 3: 14

I have been crucified with Christ; it is no
longer I who live, but Christ lives in me; and
the *life* which I now live in the flesh I live by
faith in the Son of God, who loved me and
gave Himself for me.
Galatians 2:20

Your word I have hidden in my heart, That I
might not sin against You.
Psalm 119:11

The grass withers, the flower fades, But the
word of our God stands forever.
Isaiah 40:8

Your word *is* a lamp to my feet And a light to
my path.
Psalm 119:105

But be doers of the word, and not hearers
only, deceiving yourselves.
James 1:22

Company on the Path to Clarity and Fulfillment

Each day can bring surprises and unexpected events that can cause a distracting path, but if the Woman of REACH walks with God consistently, she can maintain a firm commitment to the path God prefers.

We've all seen those winding dark roads in movie scenes. The onlookers, not the one behind the steering wheel, know what's around the unlit curve.

Not knowing can be stressful, but knowing that God's at the helm brings a sense of peace that disables the fear.

When a Woman of REACH is talking with God, praying to God, the most unexpected event can be approached and dealt with through wisdom and clarity.

Sometimes all it takes is a quiet prayer to receive clear direction; other times it may require a committed persistence to trust God in spite of what's seen or not seen.

Words of Wisdom

But You, O LORD, *are* a shield for me,
My glory and the One who lifts up my
head.
Psalm 3:3

Beloved, I pray that you may prosper in all
things and be in health, just as your soul
prospers.
3 John 1:2

Therefore, my beloved brethren, be steadfast,
immovable, always abounding in the work of
the Lord, knowing that your labor is not in
vain in the Lord.
1 Corinthians 15:58

While we do not look at the things which are
seen, but at the things which are not seen. For
the things which are seen *are* temporary, but
the things which are not seen *are* eternal.
2 Corinthians 4:18

Choosing Wisely: Four Potential Directions for Movements in Life

#1

Up—Movement that's towards God and the things of God

The upward movement in life is accompanied and fueled by a Spirit-filled life. Common features include fasting, prayer, meditation on the Word, complete dependence on and faith in God, and an understanding that all things work together for those who love the Lord and who are called according to His name. A faithful and peaceful attitude will always ride the storms of life.

#2

Down—Movement that's away from God

In this life movement, the flesh is in control. You operate out of emotions, and you are the center of your world. God is not consulted. His Word has no perceived value, and others are disregarded as God's creations; in fact, they are often viewed as a means to attaining an end—my happiness, my possessions, my wants.

#3

Left or Right—Movement that's distracting

In a chaotic world it's easy to get distracted, off schedule, interrupted in the things that concern God. The key, however, is to monitor carefully, with the guidance of the Holy Spirit, movements that may appear godly. There are times when God will have you to pause and reflect, in order to tend to issues that may need to be resolved before you can progress to a new level to fulfill the call of your vision.

Back—Movement that's familiar but not always a means to growth

The best way to explain this movement in life is for you to think back to a time, a person, or an activity that gave you immediate comfort; today, however, you know that movement might have brought temporary release from pain, from fear, or from worry, but it was clearly not in line with the life God had in mind for you. It was familiar and comfortable, but it was not supportive of your growth in the Lord.

Looking in the Mirror—Life Movements

Is there a time when you found yourself pursuing an *upward movement*, a step towards God?

It was when

Why did you do it?

What were the circumstances?

Was anyone else involved?

What was the outcome?

Is there a time when you found yourself pursuing a *downward movement*, a step away from God?

It was when

Why did you do it?

What were the circumstances?

Was anyone else involved?

What was the outcome?

Is there a time when you found yourself pursuing a *left or right movement*, a step towards distraction?

It was when

Why did you do it?

What were the circumstances?

Was anyone else involved?

What was the outcome?

Is there a time when you found yourself pursuing a *backward movement*, a step towards the familiar?

It was when

Why did you do it?

What were the circumstances?

Was anyone else involved?

What was the outcome?

Prayer Time

Go back over your responses to the *Life Movements* reflection.

As you review each one, ask God to forgive you in those areas where you did not trust Him.

Think about how those movements without Him created stumbling blocks—mental, emotional, and spiritual. Next, ask God to guide you into a place of healing, forgiveness, and where needed, correction. In this prayer, honestly tell God that you are willing to release every aspect of your life that is not in line with the Spirit-filled life He intends you to live.

And finally, ask God to create a hunger for His Word that will nourish and guide the holy and obedient life you desire to live, so that from this point forward God is a part of every movement.

Now compose a prayer that reflects your requests and then date the prayer. As we are all human, you may find the need to return to this prayer from time to time.

Lord,

Date _____

If you have been honest with the above, you are moving like a Woman of REACH who chooses to see and respond with spiritual eyes.

Words of Wisdom

"The fear of the LORD *is* the beginning of
wisdom,
An d the knowledge of the Holy One *is*
understanding.
Proverbs 9:10

And have put on the new *man* who is renewed
in knowledge according to the image of Him
who created him . . .
Colossians 3:10

Movement with Godly Purpose

In the process of the angelic ballerina reaching her highest point, there is a movement that takes her beyond her norm. It requires the ballerina to extend and move to a new level.

Movement with Godly purpose is focused, balanced, and extended—but without unnatural exertion that causes disabling side effects. It complements the heavenly dancer's grace—in other words, the ballerina's stance looks natural and appropriate.

For this movement to be successful for the Woman of REACH, she must prepare faithfully for the fulfillment of her God-given visions. Preparation is instrumental for the woman who chooses to live a life of REACH.

Words of Wisdom

I will instruct you and teach you in the way
you should go;
I will guide you with My eye.
Psalm 32:8

Inhaling a Way of Life: Habits of Life for Visionary Living

When things get out of control, what do you do? What's your stabilizing mechanism? A routine is not always a bad thing. It supports focus, commitment, and a course of action.

Have you ever reflected about some past turbulent events and discovered things that, if approached differently at the beginning, could have turned out much better and avoided many agonizing moments?

Well, a Woman of REACH learns that proactive measures are much more peaceful, satisfying, and reassuring than reactive ones that respond in an unprepared fashion to troubling situations.

It took me a while to discover the *Staying Fit for Life* pattern for living a vision-focused life, but now that I've embraced it, it's as natural as inhaling air.

While I am the first to acknowledge that there's no cookie-cutter approach for following your vision, I do encourage you to examine closely the following list of activities and then revise it to accommodate your personality and spiritual nurturing needs.

Staying Fit for Life Movements

- Pray
- Spend time in God's Word.
- Write your God-given visions down.
- *Steal away for quiet time—listen, reflect, plan, and revise.*
- Do not be jealous of anyone's success or blessings.
- Embrace every season in your life as an opportunity to become a better woman of God—to stretch your mind, to improve your attitude, to increase your love, and perfect your patience.

- Pray
- Spend time in God's Word.
- During the slow or complicated seasons of life, give yourself permission to do what you can and do not get angry when you think it's not enough.
- Encourage fellow sisters as they rise in their God-given visions.
- Praise God.
- *Steal away for quiet time—listen, reflect, plan, and revise.*
- Embrace the fact that God-given visions may come in one season, develop in another, and then come to fruition in yet another.

- Pray
- Spend time in God's Word.
- Keep a notepad close—in the car, by your bed, or in your purse—for creative insights and whispered guidance from the Holy Spirit.
- Flee from foolishness—your financial habits are important. Do you take care of your money as if there is a vision you need to support?
- Keep company with at least a few women who practice REACH.
- *Steal away for quiet time— listen, reflect, plan, and revise.*
- Seek the training, education, skills, etc. needed to fulfill your vision.
- Pray

Eva A Woman of REACH in Action

When she was 14-years-old, God planted in Eva's spirit the desire to be an evangelist. In her day, and specifically in her church, women did not take on such spiritual roles.

Eva continued to serve in her church, holding roles that were acceptable for a woman-- teaching Sunday School, serving as the president for various church groups, and speaking during church anniversary occasions.

As her college days began approaching, Eva started looking at a school that could support her dream to become an evangelist; however, when the brochures arrived from the university, Eva knew her parents could not afford the private Christian school, so she let her dream go, at least for a while.

Three academic degrees later, and standing in the college classroom where she teaches, Eva got the invitation to share the Word of God abroad. That call came after many years of experiences that had uniquely shaped Eva for this specific opportunity.

As of today, Eva has made five further trips out of the country, and she has developed a program that will bring hope and opportunity to people in need.

It may be 30 years later, but Eva's desire to share God's love in all corners of the world has come to fruition. Although the vision has been reshaped, at the age of 44 she is sharing the love of God.

Women of REACH cannot afford to give up, but they must be willing to be flexible in the pursuit of the vision.

Look in the Mirror—How are you similar or different?

Words of Wisdom

Therefore gird up the loins of your mind, be sober, and rest *your* hope fully upon the grace that is to be brought to you at the revelation of Jesus Christ; as obedient children, not conforming yourselves to the former lusts, *as* in your ignorance; but as He who called you *is* holy, you also be holy in all *your* conduct, because it is written, *"Be holy, for I am holy."*

And if you call on the Father, who without partiality judges according to each one's work, conduct yourselves throughout the time of your stay *here* in fear; knowing that you were not redeemed with corruptible things, *like* silver or gold, from your aimless conduct *received* by tradition from your fathers, but with the precious blood of Christ, as of a lamb without blemish and without spot. He indeed was foreordained before the foundation of the world, but was manifest in these last times for you who through Him believe in God, who raised Him from the dead and gave Him glory, so that your faith and hope are in God.

Since you have purified your souls in obeying the truth through the Spirit in sincere love of the brethren, love one another fervently with a pure heart, having been born again, not of corruptible seed but incorruptible, through the word of God which lives and abides forever, because
" All flesh is as grass,
And all the glory of man as the flower of the
grass.
The grass withers,
And its flower falls away,
But the word of the LORD endures forever."
1 Peter 1: 13-25

Warning

In the conception of the vision, during the preparation time periods, and during the upward movement, others may not understand your God-given vision, your efforts, nor your relationship with God. But you and God know what's taking place.

Make the unwavering decision to listen to God and to tune out the distracting chatter.

If you are keeping true to the *Staying Fit for REACH* lifestyle, then you have God's discerning voice, and you have at least a couple of like-minded friends to seek wise counsel from during the journey.

However, of even more value than the like-minded sisters in the journey, you have your chosen time alone with God. You have made God a priority, and thus His voice is a central part of the process.

Words of Wisdom

And do not be conformed to this world, but
be transformed by the renewing of your
mind, that you may prove what *is* that good
and acceptable and perfect will of God.
Romans 12:2

ATTEND TO YOUR ATTITUDE TO REPRESENT THE CHARACTER OF CHRIST

Shirley A Woman of REACH in Action

On a cool December evening, Shirley and her friend, Carrie, walked North Park Mall.

Shirley's husband, Frank, has exquisite taste, and she wanted to look at a smoker's jacket for his birthday, so they walked into a men's clothing store.

Carrie tagged behind; she hadn't known the store existed, let alone ever entered its doors. As Shirley looked at a couple of jackets, a handsome sales clerk approached. "May I help you?"

"No, we're just looking," Shirley said with a familiar smile.

As the clerk walked away, Carrie smiled awkwardly at the man. She found him most attractive. Carrie didn't know it, but Shirley had caught the look of attraction. "Would you like me to introduce you?" she asked. "Mike and I chat on occasion when I'm in the store with Frank."

"Oh no, I'm not ready." As she uttered the words, Carrie tugged on her blouse, fussed over her hair, and showcased that well-known insecure look.

"Carrie, you will never be ready if you don't change your mindset. You have to know who you belong to and who you are in Christ before others can really appreciate the beauty you possess."

"Shirley, I'm not you. You have it all together."

"No, Carrie, I don't have it all together, but I'm the daughter of the King Almighty. How can I not hold my head up high and let God shine through? I'm walking around with many gifts. My attitude regarding others and myself is a part of my testimony."

Women of REACH know their maker and what they possess at all times because of who they have chosen to follow.

Look in the Mirror—How are you similar or different?

Words of Wisdom

For You formed my inward parts;
You covered me in my mother's womb.
I will praise You, for I am fearfully *and* wonderfully
made;
Marvelous are Your works,
And *that* my soul knows very well.
My frame was not hidden from You,
When I was made in secret,
And skillfully wrought in the lowest parts of
the earth.
Your eyes saw my substance, being yet unformed.
And in Your book they all were written,
The days fashioned for me,
When *as yet there were* none of them.
Psalms 139: 13-16

But the fruit of the Spirit is love, joy, peace, longsuffering,
kindness, goodness, faithfulness, gentleness,
self-control. Against such there is no law. And
those *who are* Christ's have crucified the flesh with
its passions and desires. If we live in the Spirit, let us
also walk in the Spirit. Let us not become conceited,
provoking one another, envying one another.
Galatians 5:22-26

Addressing Attitude, Volunteers Needed:
Only the Willing Should Apply

A positive, godly, and joyful attitude should not be taken lightly. Low self-esteem or ugliness has no place in the life of a Woman of REACH. Such characteristics manifest that which is contrary to the God we serve.

There's nothing more disheartening for a woman who says she loves the Lord than to present an attitude of inferiority. And there's nothing more disgraceful than to manifest a character that makes another person feel envied, rejected, or a failure.

Such expressions not only offend the recipient, but they also illustrate fear, failure, and sometimes jealousy.

At all times, let Christ shine through. Determine to participate in God's plan each day of your life, and do it with an attitude of joy and expectation. And when the opportunity allows, make someone else's day a little brighter.

The way to do this consistently is to choose to face each waking morning with a song of praise in your heart. It does not mean every day will be filled with victories and polite and loving people, but you can rejoice in the fact that God is willing to be with you and in the fact that you choose to bring light to the lives of others.

Words of Wisdom

Now no chastening seems to be joyful for the
present, but painful; nevertheless, afterward
it yields the peaceable fruit of righteousness
to those who have been trained by it.
Hebrews 12:11

Rejoice always, pray without ceasing, in
everything give thanks; for this is the will of
God in Christ Jesus for you.
1 Thessalonians 5:16-18

Embracing the Seasons of Life

Just as the seasons change, situations in your life change as well; seasons may be self-imposed or they may occur because of events you have no control over.

Life Seasons may interrupt time schedules aimed at the achievement of visions, or they may even adjust the shape of visions—this is not a bad thing.

Seasons, if addressed with God, add maturity and sharpen your listening skills and thus your vision.

Here are a few seasonal features. Note the space provided for you to add others that may complement who you are and what you may face concerning family, employment, friends, financial standing, etc.

A Change in Income	A Parent's Need/Demands	A Disability
A New Job or the Loss of a Job	A Death in the Family	A Divorce or Bad Break Up
An Empty Nest	A New or Old Boss	
Pursuit of Education	Mounting Debt	
New Friends, Old Friends, or No Friends	A New Birth	
An Accident	Problematic Family Members	
The Needs of Children	A Brief Attack of Fear or Inadequacy	
Graduation	A Health Issue	

Looking at the seasons above:
- circle the ones that were most challenging

- place a check mark next to the ones that caused you to grow the most
- place an X next to the ones where you lost something but also gained something
- place a star next to the ones where you prayed, fasted (if your health does not permit a fast from food, abstaining from something you desire greatly may take its place), read scripture, and surrendered your will to God's Will

What have you discovered about your approach to the seasons in your life?

Words of Wisdom

And the LORD, He *is* the One who goes before you. He will be with you, He will not leave you nor forsake you; do not fear nor be dismayed."
Deuteronomy 31:8

God *is* my strength *and* power, And He makes my way perfect.
2 Samuel 22:33

And you have forgotten the exhortation which speaks to you as to sons:
"My son, do not despise the chastening of the LORD,
Nor be discouraged when you are rebuked by Him;
For whom the LORD loves He chastens,
And scourges every son whom He receives."
Hebrews 12: 5-6

Casting all your care upon Him, for He cares for you.
Be sober, be vigilant; because your adversary the devil walks about like a roaring lion, seeking whom he may devour.
1 Peter 5:7-8

Lauretta A Woman of REACH in Action

He walked out, leaving his two children, his wife and his home. He claimed the pressure was too much.

Five months later, Lauretta lost her home, was forced to relocate, and started over.

At the beginning of this distressing season, Lauretta gave herself three days to cry, then she wiped her eyes and determined to work for a better today and a better tomorrow for herself and her children.

Giving up was not an option.

Two years later, with a rented home that she had created as a cozy nest, two jobs to make ends meet, and the painful memory of a fifteen-year marriage beginning to subside in her mind, Lauretta made peace with her life. She realized that things were really more peaceful with the absence of a man who did not want his family.

Her decision to be a woman of God, a mother, and a non-bitter woman made healing possible.

Today, Lauretta smiles, and it's genuine. Her faith is stronger than it's ever been.

Women of REACH move forward in spite of the season, and while there's some giving up in the process of moving forward, what's gained is priceless if it draws a woman closer to God.

Look in the Mirror—How are you similar or different?

Words of Wisdom

So we fasted and entreated our God for this,
and He answered our prayer.
Ezra 8:23

Not that I have already attained, or am already
perfected; but I press on, that I may lay hold
of that for which Christ Jesus has also laid
hold of me.
Philippians 3:12

Amanda A Woman of REACH in Action

Some women genuinely love their jobs, and this was so true of Amanda. When she began work at a new company, she was determined to do well.

Every morning Amanda awoke asking God to let her do her best—to let creativity and wisdom work together so she could make a difference in her setting and reach the potential God had planted in her spirit. While Amanda was not the overly social-type in the workplace, she gradually became acquainted with a few people, and she engaged in light conversations from time to time.

However, the truth behind these so-called friendships came to light. One day, Amanda received an amazing opportunity—she was being promoted to a new area. This promotion was not often afforded to new arrivals. Word got around without Amanda having to say a word about the blessing. With such news, she discovered the true heart of her coworkers.

One woman confronted her: "We thought you were a nobody when you got here."

Needless to say, Amanda was hurt by the remark.

All she had done was ask God to help her do well, remain cordial and professional in the workplace, and do an outstanding job.

In spite of the initial pain, Amanda chose not to dwell on the words. She continued her journey with God and aimed to be a woman of God despite her workplace company. Over the next nine years, Amanda went from door greeter, to sales clerk, to service desk clerk, to assistant store manager, to store manager, to traveling the U.S. setting up new stores.

Women of REACH can and may have to walk alone with God.

Look in the Mirror—How are you similar or different?

Words of Wisdom

Let us therefore come boldly to the throne
of grace, that we may obtain mercy and find
grace to help in time of need.
Hebrews 4:16

Do not love the world or the things in the
world. If anyone loves the world, the love
of the Father is not in him. For all that *is* in
the world—the lust of the flesh, the lust of
the eyes, and the pride of life—is not of the
Father but is of the world.
1 John 2:15-16

Blessed *is* the man
Who walks not in the counsel of the ungodly,
Nor stands in the path of sinners,
Nor sits in the seat of the scornful;
But his delight *is* in the law of the LORD,
And in His law he meditates day and night.
He shall be like a tree
Planted by the rivers of water,
That brings forth its fruit in its season,
Whose leaf also shall not wither;
And whatever he does shall prosper.
Psalm 1:1-3

Looking in the Mirror—Weathering the Seasons

While seasons can test us, cause fatigue, and disrupt what we thought we knew and trusted, asking God for wisdom, discernment, and understanding can turn a trying season into fertile ground for positive reflection and growth.

No matter the season, God is there, unchanging. The question is, what were *you* like and who did *you* become?

Consider one of the most difficult seasons of your life.

Describe the experience:

Looking back now at this experience, and at its conclusion, how were you transformed?

At the end, were you a better person, a stronger model for others enduring a similar season, a more faithful believer, or did you become rebellious, angry, depressed, etc.?

Words of Wisdom

These things I have spoken to you, that in Me
you may have peace. In the world you will
have tribulation; but be of good cheer, I have
overcome the world."
John 16:33

And not only *that,* but we also glory in tribulations,
knowing that tribulation produces
perseverance; and perseverance, character;
and character, hope.
Romans 5:3-4

Dressing for the Journey: Get Ready, Get Ready

A beautiful woman on the inside, changed and renewed by the Word, desires to be just as beautiful on the outside.

Given the occasion, she selects an outfit that is stylish yet functional. The wrong outfit can stifle

participation and can shout clearly to observers that this woman is unprepared and uninformed.

A Woman of REACH with a godly attitude must gird herself. The word "gird" means to prepare for action, to equip. Woman of REACH have a mission, for which they must be fully prepared.

In 1 Samuel 17, Saul attempts to prepare David for battle. He gives him armor as an act of assistance, but it does not work for David, who disrobes and selects that which is more fitting for him and his mission.

Every woman must clothe herself to REACH. While some garment features will be common among godly women, individual visions and personalities will shape unique differences in a REACHer's attire.

Words of Wisdom

Therefore take up the whole armor of God,
that you may be able to withstand in the evil
day, and having done all, to stand.
Stand therefore, having girded your waist
with truth, having put on the breastplate of
righteousness, and having shod your feet with
the preparation of the gospel of peace; above
all, taking the shield of faith with which you
will be able to quench all the fiery darts of the
wicked one. And take the helmet of salvation,
and the sword of the Spirit, which is the word
of God;
Ephesians 6:13-17

Eva's Apparel

A three-piece ensemble:

- First, Eva's feet are covered in education. It took her years to acquire her degrees, but education is a part of her being, formal and informal. She knows she will be a student for life.

- Second, Eva's outer robe appears as follows: scripture threads through every seam; faith, endurance, and patience serve as a yoke around her collar; creativity covers her breast; determination and fearlessness patch the elbows; hope covers her back; and prayer runs right across a gold inlay that meets at her knees.

- Finally, Eva wears a seamless gown underneath the robe, and a matching scarf forms a neatly tied bow right above her forehead. The ensemble is made of fine humility silk and complements the fully extended position of REACH. One key thing to note— before Eva robes in the matching pieces, she always takes two hours to soak in a bath of quiet solitude. She wants every inch of her skin prepared for the garment that will yield her gifts in the season of full extension of her vision.

Eva knows her vision well, and she's adorned herself to meet stages of preparation, reflection, testing, and then living the vision God has birthed in her.

Words of Wisdom

Therefore, as *the* elect of God, holy and beloved, put on tender mercies, kindness, humility, meekness, longsuffering; bearing with one another, and forgiving one another, if anyone has a complaint against another; even as Christ forgave you, so you also *must do*. Above all these things put on love, which is the bond of perfection. And let the peace of God rule in your hearts, to which also you were called in one body; and be thankful. Let the word of Christ dwell in you richly in all wisdom, teaching and admonishing one another in psalms and hymns and spiritual songs, singing with grace in your hearts to the Lord. And *whatever* you do in word or deed, *do* all in the name of the Lord Jesus, giving thanks to God the Father through Him.
Colossians 3:12-17

Designer at Work

Today, you are a designer, and you have been commissioned to design your attire as a Woman of REACH.

Design the garment that will adorn your mind, heart, and body as you are accomplishing the vision God has given you. Even for those visions that have not been revealed, it's not too early to start preparing. We know the basic characteristics of God, and His desires for us will not work against His nature.

Sketch out your adornment and label key features; remember to keep God's Word in mind as you prepare to be a woman of God-given vision.

Before you get started, go back to the vision you noted and explored during the brainstorming activity.

Given the people, activities, challenges, etc. you might face, what has to be a part of your garment?

Find a clean working space and assemble the materials you'll need. Consider:
- an attitude of hope
- a mind of creativity
- a heart of love
- a large clean sheet of paper
- colored markers, pens, pencils, and crayons
- your Bible
- other inspirational, spiritually related reading material

Sketch out a garment that suits you and then label the unique features. Review Eva's three-piece garment to get some ideas.

Your Canvas

Words of Wisdom

For though we walk in the flesh, we do not
war according to the flesh. For the weapons
of our warfare *are* not carnal but mighty in
God for pulling down strongholds, casting
down arguments and every high thing that
exalts itself against the knowledge of God,
bringing every thought into captivity to the
obedience of Christ . .
2 Corinthians 10:3-5

But the fruit of the Spirit is love, joy, peace,
longsuffering, kindness, goodness, faithfulness,
gentleness, self-control. Against such
there is no law.
Galatians 5:22-23

Side by Side

Take a look at your garment and the labels you have placed on your outfit.
Now look at God's characteristics.

Do you need to add, delete, or change some features so that you are in
line with God's nature?

Response:

Words of Wisdom

You are of God, little children, and have
overcome them, because He who is in you is
greater than he who is in the world.
1 John 4:4

There is no fear in love; but perfect love casts
out fear, because fear involves torment. But
he who fears has not been made perfect in
love. We love Him because He first loved us.
1 John 4:18-19

And have put on the new *man* who is renewed
in knowledge according to the image of Him
who created him.
Colossians 3:10

CHOOSE TO ABANDON FEAR BECAUSE GOD IS MIGHTIER THAN ANY OPPOSITION

Venus A Woman of REACH in Action

It was getting close to the trip. One morning, when Venus was leaving work, a small voice said, "What do you think you're doing? You're not equipped for this."

That voice was speaking to the gift Venus had given herself.

All her life she had wanted to write a novel, but with work, family, and all the other demands, that book never seemed to make it to the page.

At fifty, Venus knew she was not getting any younger and that if she never carved out the time to explore this burning desire, it would not happen.

When Venus heard the voice, it was two weeks before her trip to Spain, the setting for her Christian fiction novel.

For less than thirty seconds, that defeating, lying voice had the floor, but when that thirty seconds passed Venus said, "Hush, you are a liar. This is for me."

Venus took her trip and praised God for giving her the opportunity. She's now back in the States, completing the second revision of the book, and she's determined that most of the proceeds will put her in a position to help God's people on a fulltime basis.

Women of REACH recognize the lies of deception, and they go after their visions armed with the guidance of the Holy Spirit.

Look in the Mirror—How are you similar or different?

Rejecting the Tricolor Shawl of Fear

What is Satan after?

He wants what God has intended for you—God's will for your life, your joy, and your peace.

The Bible says we are not fighting against flesh and blood, but against powers and principalities, and, trust me, these can come well dressed, in an attire of humbleness and kindness, and with some of the most intellectual sounding rhetoric you have ever heard.

What is key to understanding is that lies and deception will attach themselves both to knowing and to unknowing people. These people will be used to defeat you through deeds and words. The same people will challenge your thoughts if you leave them unguarded from the foolishness and faithlessness of this world.

For visionary women, there are three warning signs for the approach of fear:

First, when you lean only on your own strength through the journey, you are opening the door to fear. There's a reason why God takes us through tests and trying times. It's to build us up through Him. Consequently, you need to learn to heed trying times with a heart of repentance and acceptance; doing so will prepare you for the tasks forthcoming. In these situations, you are walking in God's strength, handmade by God.

When we lose sight of God and of what we are doing for His people, we have by co-participation invited fear into the vision—where it has no place because the vision belongs to God. We are simply its custodians.

Second, when you begin feeling stretched by the journey and begin questioning if you made the right decision in pursuing the vision, know that you are opening the door to fear. Vision living is not easy, and I don't know of too many mature, godly people who haven't felt stretched and fearful from time to time.

But don't allow the fear to overtake your life or your vision. Feeling stretched when you encounter more than you bargained for is normal. Always remember, though, that God doesn't give you the complete picture ahead of time, however finished as you may think the picture is as you get closer and closer to the destination. As a woman who battles daily with control, I've yet to find the vision as I expected. Embracing creativity and flexibility are central to continued joy in vision living.

So, attempting to deny that the call was from God opens the door to doubt, and doubt leads to fear. It took me a while to grasp this principle. What turned things around for me was when I began appreciating and praising God for the stretching moments—attitude made a lot of difference. I also realized that what used to be very tiring emotionally and physically had become a lighter burden, and the testing periods moved a lot quicker. The key was coupling prayer and faith in God's wisdom for what I was encountering.

Finally, when you begin, without guard, to absorb the thoughts of the naysayers, you are opening the door to fear. You will doubtless get a number of tips about your vision and how you should proceed or why you should not proceed. These encounters you cannot escape; however, how you receive this information and what you do with it is totally in your hands.

When I was a novice at REACH, I absorbed much more than I should have. However, as I became a living practitioner of *Staying Fit for Life Movements* (revisit the list), and as the naysayers moved in and out of my vision journey, I was able to listen with a more discerning ear.

I rarely silenced anyone because my spirit had a guard so well equipped that I knew when their advice was appropriate for my consideration.

Trust me, God is able to use some of the most interesting individuals and ideas for His plan, but you have got to let the Holy Spirit guide you into this understanding.

As a final point, be mindful of who you share your vision with, particularly the intimate details. Not everyone's equipped to handle what God has called you to. Besides, if you are a practitioner of *Staying Fit for Life Movements*, you will have Women of REACH in your circle to be sounding boards and prayer warriors.

Words of Wisdom

The LORD *is* my light and my salvation;
Whom shall I fear?
The LORD *is* the strength of my life;
Of whom shall I be afraid?
Psalm 27:1

Erin A Woman of REACH in Action

Erin taught at a well-respected university in Houston, Texas. However, towards the end of her second year, she felt the Lord calling her to go to seminary school.

This wasn't a bad thing at all because Erin always knew that she would serve the Lord in a unique way and that preparation was a part of the journey.

She had a challenging decision to make, however. Should she leave her university position after taking many years to get her doctorate and downgrade to a part-time position at a two-year college in order to earn the money to go to seminary school full-time?

Erin had not made up her mind to pursue the degree, until a friend at church encouraged her to apply to the seminary school that she had attended.

Erin thought about applying and decided that it would not hurt to see if she would be accepted.

In the meantime, she expressed her ideas to a few colleagues at the university where she taught. They were not fans at all.

All three seemed to blurt out their ideas at once.

"Why would you want to teach at a community college? You have a Ph.D."

"I think you would be making a big mistake; you just finished your degree and you are going to start over?"

"It sounds to me like you're trying to recapture something from your youth. You're a grown woman, and you need to let this foolishness go."

Erin immediately realized she had made a mistake in sharing. But she did not allow her friends to persuade her to abandon the possibility of seminary school.

The next week, Erin was attending a conference in Chicago, and she decided to take some of that time in her hotel room to pray over the matter and seek God's discerning voice.

It was the first night of the conference, and, instead of attending the opening event activities, Erin planted herself next to her bed, on her knees, with her Bible in front of her. During her undergraduate degree, a good friend had given her key verses to read during trying times. These passages had come from her friend's grandmother.

Erin began to read Psalm 86. She read it over and over. Then she quietly called out to God in prayer.

Next, she read Psalm 37 in its entirety. After that reading, she then prayed more passionately to God, asking Him to shape those desires in her heart and to guide her in a joy that would bring Him glory and praise. At that very moment, Erin had complete peace about leaving her job at the university.

When Erin returned home, she found not only an acceptance letter from the seminary, but also an awards letter for a tuition-free scholarship.

The next year was not an easy journey; in fact, God whispered to Erin, during another prayer time, that things were not going to turn out the way Erin expected.

At the time, Erin didn't know what that meant, but she was at peace with the words.

Did Erin finish the seminary degree?

No.

Did she end up teaching full-time at a community college? Yes.

Did the teaching opportunity lead to more opportunities to share the Word of God in the U.S. and

beyond?

Yes.

Did Erin finally understand that the vision of ministry wasn't turning out *the way she expected* with a seminary degree under her belt, and was she accepting of the revised vision?

Absolutely yes!

Women of REACH do not fear the journey and what it brings; they depend on God to lead and protect.

Look in the Mirror—How are you similar or different?

Words of Wisdom

For God has not given us a spirit of fear, but
of power and of love and of a sound mind.
1 Timothy 1:7

HOLD THE NEEDS OF OTHERS IN VIEW BECAUSE IT'S NOT ALL ABOUT YOU

Barbara A Woman of REACH in Action

Barbara had been working at her present job for about two years before she finally found some comfort conversing with her supervisor.

Barbara's personality is a little reserved. She wasn't always like this, but over the years she'd met more people who had turned on her, betrayed her, or simply faked a friendship.

Barbara had vowed not to trust anyone too quickly. But one day, the Holy Spirit spoke to Barbara. Pointedly, the Spirit said, "It's not all about you."

That was all Barbara needed to hear. Yes, she needed to guard her heart, but she had to see people's actions as manifestations of where they were in their walk with Christ.

Barbara realized that those who had wounded her had caused her to hide. She also realized that her actions and her prayers were of far greater importance than her wounded feelings. She needed to become more than a wounded Christian hiding from those who needed her.

It was after those informing words from the Holy Spirit that Barbara began to chat with her supervisor. This led to praying for him and then witnessing with her life, which began to lead to her supervisor's changed character.

Over the next two years, Barbara found her supervisor not only asking Barbara to pray for him, but even asking Barbara to chat with his daughter about some serious spiritual issues.

When Barbara held the needs of others above her own personal comfort, she was able to touch an entire family and workplace.

Women who REACH understand their realm of influence.

Look in the Mirror—How are you similar or different?

Words of Wisdom

Therefore, to him who knows to do good and
does not do *it,* to him it is sin.
James 4:17

And let us not grow weary while doing good,
for in due season we shall reap if we do not
lose heart.
Galatians 6:9

Beloved, let us love one another, for love is
of God; and everyone who loves is born of
God and knows God.
1 John 4:7

And be kind to one another, tenderhearted,
forgiving one another, even as God in Christ
forgave you.
Ephesians 4:32

The Bigger Purpose is Vision Living: A Call from God

Women of REACH help others. It's simply what we do.

People in need may be in your own backyard; they may sit with you at lunch, or they may be thousands of miles away in another country.

When you take on the call to live out a God-given vision, the realm of that influence could, unbeknown to yourself, be of great magnitude.

Let me share some excerpts from a message I gave to an audience of ministers and lay servants.

Here's the crux of my point—our vision is rooted in the unequivocal and undeniable yielding to God's personal call on our lives. At this moment every individual in this room who is a believer has been singly and collectively called out. *Our call is* to continually reach out and nurture hope.

As believers, our call embraces a body of people we may or may not be intimately aware of, but God is. Our single-minded focus should be that our call meets the needs and concerns of a hurting, distraught, and confused humanity.

Ask yourselves this: to fall short in your call is to hurt whom, surrender what to whom, to stop what from occurring?

You must answer this question honestly.

While you ponder over your own answer, let me review briefly a few biblical examples of those who met the call:

Rahab: a prostitute, a scar on society, but when the time came, she was the way in; she was the answer. Rahab did not give up; she gave in and thus secured a home for herself and her family and a future with God. She was not selfish; she was willing, although it was dangerous. Hope was secured.

Ruth: widowed, a foreigner to her own family, and one who ultimately lost all but her mother-in-law was yet loyal, committed, obedient, and faithful. She fulfilled the call to meet her mother-in-law's needs. Ruth had hope that life with Naomi and her God would be a better life than the one she had left behind. The Hope for Ruth's offspring was secured.

Mordecai: stepfather, visionary, guide, counselor, took Esther and placed her in a position and then a path that would save the Jews yet again. Hope was secured.

Esther: orphan girl, least likely although beautiful, obeyed the rules, but when the time came embraced fasting and, down on her knees, sought God's wisdom to turn an almost impossible situation around. Hope for the Jews was secured.

And finally, my favorite, Paul: studious, legalistic at first, but by the end spiritually wise, committed, compassionate—a sounding voice for the early church, a legacy for today's church, and a model for visionary people. Hope was secured.

Notice what's common among all these who I assert secured hope—it was the fact that they honored the call or that defining moment that would impact more than just *themselves*.

To fall short in our vision is to hurt whom, surrender what to whom, to stop what from occurring?

Yes, your vision may seem hard to believe because it stems from our Heavenly Father, yet it is grounded in the realization and daily awareness that Jesus *is* and thus your vision can be *fulfilled*.

Fulfill the call and secure the hope for the countless ones God has destined to be blessed by your obedience in embracing your vision.

Baby's Breath

Imagine a beautiful vase filled with white baby's breath and five long stemmed roses peeking out from between the clusters of baby's breath. Eventually those roses are going to wither, turn brown, and discolor the arrangement. Well, if you know anything about baby's breath, you know it has a sustaining presence of beauty—it will outlast almost any flower in its company.

Choose to be that cluster of baby's breath. Brighten your setting with beauty and joy as you
fulfill your call.

Recognize who you are and celebrate God's gift in you by extending kindness, concern, and God's love to others. Do not wait until the call is fulfilled. Follow the call by presenting yourself as baby's breath to those around you.

Begin with this very practical suggestion:

Make a list of three friends, acquaintances, or coworkers, and extend an act of kindness just because God is love and you are God's. Then

- send a card
- make a call
- bake a batch of cookies
- send some flowers
- lend a helping hand
- devote a day of prayer

Bring unexpected kindness to someone's life.

Try to get in the habit of waking in the mornings and asking God who you should bless. Be
observant in your surroundings, looking for that someone who hungers for a little joy. Finally, try to be giving, at least in prayer and try to present a kind attitude to those who seem to be the most hateful, ugly, or offensive. They need the light more than anyone, even though they are the most challenging.

As I write these words, I, too, am compelled to reiterate the need to seek the Holy Spirit's guidance, especially in acts of kindness. Let God point you in the direction you should travel and toward the company you should keep.

Siva A Woman of REACH in Action

Siva is a single mother, and she has often prayed the prayers in the *Power of a Praying Parent.*

However, one day a friend from her past came back into her life. She had known this man about thirty years ago, but they had not stayed in contact. What reignited their friendship was the passing of his brother. Siva made a call to extend her condolences. A few months went by, and she heard that he was going through some relationship problems, so she made that second call to give words of encouragement.

Another several months passed, and Siva was awakened at 2:00 a.m. in the morning to pray for her son. She got out of her bed, went into the living room, and placed herself prostrate on the floor. As she concluded her intercessory prayer and began to rise to go back to her bed, the Lord placed her old friend on her heart, but this was more than just a friendly reminder that he needed prayer. God was calling Siva to intercede for this man.

By the time Siva got back to her bed, she knew she would begin a 40-day fast that included no food from midnight until 5:00 p.m. and a commitment of daily prayer for a man who was little more than a stranger. But she would stand as intercessor for him, praying the prayers found in the *Power of a Praying Parent.*

Making the choice to stand as intercessor for someone is a demanding surrender. You give yourself as you pour out your spirit. Yet Siva knew that if she was really a child of God, she should be living her life daily to aid her sisters and brothers in Christ.

Siva chose to put the needs of someone else before her own personal comfort, and for the next forty days she prayed for this man to bring him a peace and love he had never experienced.

Women of REACH yield to the needs of others.

Look in the Mirror—How are you similar or different?

Words of Wisdom

And I will pray the Father, and He will give
you another Helper, that He may abide with
you forever—the Spirit of truth, whom the
world cannot receive, because it neither sees
Him nor knows Him; but you know Him, for
He dwells with you and will be in you.
John 14:16-17

Closing

Dear Sisters,

Our time in this book has come to an end. I hope you have enjoyed the journey. I certainly have. As I began the book with an opportunity for you to get to know me, I want to conclude the same way. It's one thing to give you advice on how to prepare and live out the visions God has birthed in you. It's another to show that I have taken the advice as well. But, this is exactly what I want to do.

When I finished my first degree in business, I went into management with Wal-Mart Stores, Inc. However, towards the end of my seventh year, I had a longing to be in school. I wanted to write, speak, and teach. Well, before I took that leap into an English graduate program, I did some investigation. I wanted to know what I was getting into, and I wanted to know how to be successful. So, what did I do? I talked to the experts. I interviewed and surveyed those who were doing what God had placed in my spirit. Trust me, this was a God-thing. For me to try

graduate school (in a time when Internet classes were not an option) meant I would have to leave a well paying career as a single mother totally responsible for the financial care of my child and myself.

Yet the desire to help people as an educator, speaker, and writer was more pressing than the need to stay employed full-time for what would be—though at the time I didn't know this—the next six years of my life. Long before the book *REACH* became known to me, God was guiding me through the process. Now, let me be clear; I'm not suggesting that anyone leave a job. Your journey with God is your own—there's no cookie-cutter pattern to follow. I cannot reiterate this enough.

Before each major move in my life has occurred, it's been preceded with prayer and with listening to God's voice. Oftentimes I had to seclude myself for a day or two to reflect and pray—to clearly hear God's voice and to shut out the world's expectations, standards, and comments. Once I had confirmation, I would proceed by investigating the new terrain in a number of ways and creating a feasible, flexible plan.

Once I was engaged in the various phases of my vision, I again took time alone to reflect on my journey, staying in hotels in small towns with only the basics and my Bible or going to the house of a girlfriend who would allow me the time alone I needed with God. Be assured, at times I questioned certain outcomes; I questioned my own ability to do well (especially if I felt I was failing in some area); and I would even ask if I were doing these things solely for. However, the Spirit guided me into accepting my journey and all I was going through as growing opportunities—a changed attitude does wonders.

One more thing, and maybe the most important: God, all throughout my journey of the God-given vision, placed godly people in key places who counseled, supported, and opened unexpected doors. There is one person in particular who deserves my sincere thanks. His name is Robb Jackson, a man of God who encouraged me, guided me, and corrected me during many phases of my journey. As I look back, I can see that Robb greeted me at the start of my vision and has been a counselor ever since.

Many times those God placed in my path did not know how they had been worked into the master plan. Was it all easy? No. Has it all been worth it? Yes.

What follows next, in Appendix A, is a portrait of my academic career that has supported my teaching, writing, and speaking in an array of settings. If you look closely, you can see where I took time to prepare, where I stretched myself, where I placed myself in the company of like-minded people, and even, if you really look closely, where down seasons allowed time for reflection and renewal.

What's not recorded are the dates and places where I rested on my knees crying out to God because I was tired, lonely, or doubting my choices; the times where great sacrifices took a toll on my family; the countless times when I had to confront those who questioned what I was doing; and the many, many times I cried tears of joy because I knew it was God working in me to complete all that I have and will do for Him. As you review my Curriculum Vitae (CV) in Appendix A, consider documenting your own journey.

Yours may not look like mine if you are not planning to be an educator, writer, or speaker, but you should have areas devoted to investigation, preparation, reflection, and participation that complement your vision and what you need to live that vision.

Finally, as I have made additions to my CV over the years, I have thought about how I would have so appreciated such an example when I was eighteen, hungry to do so much, but so directionless. What I know now is that God has used my experiences to help others. I now serve as an example and a means of hope for others who may be pregnant with a vision but as yet directionless.

It is my prayer, however, that after reading *REACH* you have an example of how to excel in your God-given visions.

Your Sister in Christ,
Avis

Words of Wisdom

And do not be conformed to this world, but
be transformed by the renewing of your
mind, that you may prove what *is* that good
and acceptable and perfect will of God.
Romans 12:2

Taking a Practical Approach—A Second Look

For one of those God-given visions, what practical activities do you see supporting achievement?

List the activities you will have to complete to live the vision. Consider training, academic classes, volunteer work, reading materials, organizational membership, collaborations, mentoring, networking, etc.

Consider the attitude adjustments, areas where discipline is required, or habits you need to cease. All of these efforts will support your complete engagement in the vision.

Next, consider your resources or support team. For some, it may be the Trinity alone. For others, there may be a friend or two who become people of *REACH* and who can help you in the journey as you trust in the Trinity.

Appendix B provides working space for you to begin drafting steps to help you see more clearly the means for living out your God-given vision. Now remember, above all other, praying, trusting, and reading the scriptures are necessities.

The vision God has given you is important and requires your commitment.

Enjoy the journey, my sisters, and may God be with you every step of the way.

Words of Wisdom

Do not be deceived, God is not mocked; for whatever a man sows, that he will also reap. For he who sows to his flesh will of the flesh reap corruption, but he who sows to the Spirit will of the Spirit reap everlasting life. And let us not grow weary while doing good, for in due season we shall reap if we do not lose heart.
Galatians 6:7-9

Appendix A: Curriculum Vitae

Academic Preparation

Master of Arts in Organizational Management with an International Focus, Ashford University Online Program, Clinton, Iowa, May 2010

Logsdon School of Theology, Corpus Christi, TX, Extension Site (2000, 2002-2003) and Perkins School of Theology (2003) Graduate Courses (48 hours Total)

Ph.D. in Rhetoric and Writing, Bowling Green State University, Ohio, August 1999

The Bread Loaf School of English, Middlebury, Vermont, July-August 1996

Master of Arts in English, Texas A&M University-Corpus Christi, Corpus Christi, TX, May 1996

Bachelor of Business Administration, University of North Texas, Denton, TX, December 1984

Global Projects

Literacy Project , Funds for Papua New Guinea, Fall 2008

Fulbright Researcher, Senegal, West Africa, June 2nd-30th, 2006

Rome Studies English Professor, Italy, Fall 2005 and Fall 2006

Seminar Facilitator, Namibia, Africa (South Africa), July 2005

Rome Studies English Professor, Guest Lecturer, "The New Testament and English Writers in Italy," Venice, Florence, and Rome, Italy, Fall 2004

Women of Afghanistan Fund Raiser, Guest Speaker, Corpus Christi, TX, November 2001

Employment History

Educator Experience

Religion and English Professor, North Lake College, Irving, TX, 2004 – January 2010

Adjunct English Instructor, Cedar Valley College, Lancaster, TX, and Tarrant County Junior College, Fort Worth, TX, Fall 2003

Assistant Professor of English, Texas A&M University-Corpus Christi, Corpus Christi, TX, August 1999-August 2002

Graduate Teaching Assistant, General Studies Writing Program, Bowling Green State University, Bowling Green, OH, August 1998-May 1999

Teaching Consultant, Center for Teaching, Learning, & Technology, Bowling Green State University, Bowling Green, OH, July 1997-July 1998

Graduate Teaching Consultant, General Studies Writing Program, Bowling Green State University, Bowling Green, OH, August 1996-May 1997

Instructor, English Writing Lab, Del Mar College, Corpus Christi, TX, May-June 1996

Instructor, Basic Business Courses, Platt Career School, Corpus Christi, TX, 1984

Substitute Teacher, Public Schools, Corpus Christi Independent School District and Calallen Independent School District, Corpus Christi, TX, 1984-1985

Related Teaching Experience

Facilitator, Upward Bound Program Workshop—"Securing Your Vision with an Attitude of REACH," North Lake College, Irving, TX, April 25, 2009

Guest Lecturer, Leadership Institute—"Professionalism, Considering the Context," North Lake College, Irving, TX, Spring 2008

Facilitator, Upward Bound Program Workshop—"Critical Thinking," North Lake College, Irving, TX, Spring 2006

Facilitator, TRIO Workshop—"Reading Critically and Note Taking," North Lake College, Irving, TX, Spring 2005

Guest Lecturer, Career Services Seminar—"Professionalism in the Workplace," North Lake College, Irving, TX, Sept. 2005

Peer Collaboration Workshop Fellow, Texas A&M University—Corpus Christi, Corpus Christi, TX, Fall 2001

Facilitator, ExCET Prep Review Workshop, Texas A&M University—Corpus Christi, Corpus Christi, TX, August 2001

Facilitator, ExCET Prep Review Workshop, Texas A&M University—Corpus Christi, Corpus Christi, TX, April 2001

Co-Leader with Susan Loudermilk, ExCET Prep Review Workshop, Texas A&M University—Corpus Christi, Corpus Christi, TX, September 2000

Co-Leader with Vanessa Jackson, ExCET Prep Review Workshop, Texas A&M University—Corpus Christi, Corpus Christi, TX, February 2000

Guest Speaker, "Ethnography and Writing," English 5345—Chicano Literature and Language, Texas A&M University—Corpus Christi, Corpus Christi, TX, Spring 2000

Guest Speaker, "Teaching Writing," English 5372—Composition Theory and Pedagogy, Texas A&M University—Corpus Christi, Corpus Christi, TX, Spring 2000

Researcher Experience

Researcher, Daily Travel Experiences in Italy, May 2007—To Support a Christian Fiction Novel

Researcher, Christian Women in Senegal West, Africa: Living Out a Practical Faith as the Minority Religion, 2006—A Lecture for Logsdon School of Theology, the Site campus in Corpus Christi, TX

Researcher, Families Studying a Country Together: Embracing Global Preparation, 2006—A Guide and Forum for African American and Hispanic Families

Researcher, Ethnographic Observation Project with Public School Language Arts Teachers, Corpus Christi, TX, February-May 2000—A Presentation for Public School Teachers

University Liaison, BRITE (Building Relationships in Technology and Education) Bowling Green State University and the Toledo Schools, Spring 1997—A Presentation for Public School Teachers

Writing Coach, Collaborative project between Texas A&M University— Corpus Christi and The Nueces County Juvenile Center, January 1996–May 1997—A Community Service Project

College and University Administrative Experience

Religion Coordinator, North Lake College, Irving, TX, Fall 2007-November 2009

Event Coordinator, Religion Panel Presentation: "Religion and the Obscure," North Lake College, Irving, TX, September 2007

Event Coordinator, Celebration of Womanhood, A Woman's History Event, North Lake College, Irving, TX, March 2004, March 2005, March 2006, and March 2007

English Coordinator, North Lake College, Irving, TX, Spring 2005 and Fall 2005

Undergraduate English Coordinator, Texas A&M University—Corpus Christi, Corpus Christi, TX, 2001-2002

University Author's Day Coordinator, Texas A&M University—Corpus Christi, Corpus Christi, TX, March 2002

Young Author's Writing Camp Director, Texas A&M University—Corpus Christi, Corpus Christi, TX, Summer 2001

Program Developer, Communication Triad, Texas A&M University—Corpus Christi, Corpus Christi, TX, Spring-Summer 2000

Administrative Assistant, Center for Teaching, Learning & Technology, Bowling Green State University, Bowling Green, OH, May 1998 – July 1998

Daedalus Administrator, First-year Writing Program, Texas A&M University—Corpus Christi, Corpus Christi, TX, October 19994- August 1995

Placement Reader, First-year Writing Program, Texas A&M University—Corpus Christi, Corpus Christi, TX, August 1995

Managerial Experience

Wal-Mart Stores Inc., 1985-1993
> *Store Manager*, Retail Division
> *Store Planning Assistant*, Store Planning Division
> *Assistant Store Manager*, Retail Division
> *Assistant Wholesale Club Manager*, Sam's Club Division

Highland Appliance Stores, 1984
> *Assistant Office Manager*

Writing Opportunities

Grants

$10,000--"Having Fun and Learning: The Writing Process in an Author's Camp Setting"

> Partnership for Texas Public Schools Regent's Initiative Collaborative Research Grant, 2001–2002. The grant supported writing camps hosted on the Texas A&M University—Corpus Christi campus. Elementary aged children, graduate students, and public school teachers participated.

$10,000—"A Language Arts Writer/Reader/Performance Camp: What Happens to Learning

> When We Look at Biology from Multiple Perspectives? Partnership for Texas Public Schools Regent's Initiative Collaborative Research Grant, 2000-2001. The grant supported group learning activities between Education and English, Science professors and elementary and high school level students as well as their teachers.

$4,215—"Students and Teachers as Writing Ethnographers: Meeting and Exceeding the Expectations of the State of Texas"

University Grant Awarded for Spring 2001. The grant supported the collaboration between public school teachers and a college professor. Participants investigated the use of ethnographic practices in the teaching of writing in view of state mandated expectations.

$1,487—"Technography: Uncovering Ethnography in the Technical Writing Process"

A CESAR Grant Co-Awarded for 2000-2001 school year. The grant supported the research of technical writing classes that employed ethnographic practices in the teaching of technical communication.

$235—"Advanced Composition, WAC, and Technology: Building Technology Responsible Ties"

A CADTL Grant awarded Spring 2000. The grant supported a presentation at the Computers and Writing Conference in Fort Worth, TX.

Publications

Book, A Collection of Short Stories. Work in Progress.

Devotional, *The Fruits of Solitude & Silence.* Work in Progress.

Book, *Doors toward Destiny*, Forthcoming

Book, *El Sendero Para Ser Una Mujer Visionaria de Dios*, Westbow Press, Late Sumer, 2010

Book, *REACH*, Xulon Press, 2009

Article. "Managing Groups with a Lens toward Global Participation": Submitted 2008 for Publication Review

Article, Co-authored. "Using Ethnographic Research Practices for Technical Writing Assignments: Developing a Manual for Employees," *Business Communication Quarterly,* July 2002

Book Review, *Technical Writing: A Practical Approach*, *Technical Communication,* May 2002

Book Review, *Technical English: Writing, Reading, and Speaking, Journal of Technical Communication*, May 2002

Book Review, *Comp Tales. English Journal*, May 2001

Book Review, *Writing in the Real World, English Journal,* May 2001

Book Review, *Strategies for Struggling Writers. English Journal,* March 1999

Book Review, *A World's Fair for the Global Village, Computer Mediated Communication Magazine* 1Dec.1997. <http://www.december.com/cmc/mag/current/toc.html>

College/University Service

Committees

Hiring Committee, North Lake College, College Counselor, Fall 2007

Hiring Committee, North Lake College, Speech Visiting Scholar, Spring 2007

Hiring Committee, North Lake College, Rome Art Faculty Member, Spring 2006

Continuing Education Committee, North Lake College, Fall 2005-2009

Hiring Committee, North Lake College, Math and Science Dean, Spring 2005

Hiring Committee, Texas A&M University—Corpus Christi, Two Tenure-track English positions, 2001-2002

Outreach Council, Advisory Board for University Outreach, Texas A&M University—Corpus Christi, 2001 – 2002

Chair, Library Committee, Texas A&M University—Corpus Christi, 2001-2002

Undergraduate Studies Committee, Texas A&M University—Corpus Christi, 2001-2002

English Coordinating Committee, Texas A&M University—Corpus Christi, 2001-2002

Haas Awards Committee, Texas A&M University—Corpus Christi, 2000-2002

Hiring Committee, Texas A&M University—Corpus Christi, Multiple Tenure-track English positions, Spring 2000 (Attended the MLA Conference in Washington DC to interview potential applicants)

Library Committee, English Department Representative, Texas A&M University—Corpus Christi, Fall 1999 – 2002

SAC Program Assessment Review of English 1302, Texas A&M University—Corpus Christi, Fall 1999

Hiring Committee, Bowling Green State University, Professor, Scientific and Technical Communication, 1998

Hiring Committee, Bowling Green Slate University, Professor, English-Education, 1996-1997

CTLT (Center for Teaching, Learning and Technology) Advisory Board, Bowling Green State University, 1997–1997

Advising

ExCET Coordinator, Texas A&M University--Corpus Christi, 2000–2002

Undergraduate English Student Advisor, Texas A&M University—Corpus Christi, Spring 2001-2002

Graduate English Student Advisor, Texas A&M University—Corpus Christi, Fall 2000-2002

African American Culture Society Advisor, Texas A&.M University—Corpus Christi, Spring 2000

Mentoring Activities

Freshman Orientation Leader, Texas A&M University—Corpus Christi, Summer 1995
- Served as a mentor and guide for first—year students

Peer Educator, Student Life Services, Texas A&M University—Corpus Christi, Spring 1994
- Served as a facilitator for student group discussions

Appointments

Texas A&M University System Institute for School-University Partnerships—Academy Representative 2000-2002

Community Service

Speeches

Professional Development Speaker, Student Enrollment and Development Department, North Lake College, "The Pursuit of Excellence: A Choice, Not a Command," April 2006

Event Speaker, Professional Support Staff Holiday Luncheon, North Lake College, "The Ultimate Gift List," December 2005

Guest Speaker, Northgate United Methodist Church, Irving, TX, "Experiencing Namibia, Africa," August 2005

Guest Speaker, Arcadia Park United Methodist Church, Dallas, TX, "We Have Choices in the Way We Respond" November 2004

Keynote Speaker, MOP Mothers of Preschoolers, Corpus Christi, "We are Walking Reflections," February 11, 2003

Panel Presenter, Roy Miller High School, Corpus Christi, "Youth Groups: The Purpose from a Member's Perspective," February 8, 2003

Panel Presenter, First Baptist Church, Corpus Christi, "The Importance of Religious Education," February 4, 2003

Keynote Speaker, Tuloso-Midway Middle School, Corpus Christi, TX, "Thinking Positively: Succeeding Not only on State Exams but also in Life," February

Key Note Speaker, Sigma Tau Delta, Initiation Ceremony of the English Honor Society, "The Journey to Becoming What You Want," November 1, 2001

Guest Lecturer, "The Recipe for Impact (A Commitment to Character and Excellence): A 5 Step Process for Middle School Students" Haas Middle School, May 2001

Guest Speaker, Black History Month Celebration: A Walk with African Americans, West Oso High School, Corpus Christi, February 23, 2001

Key Note Speaker Black History Month Assembly, West Oso High School, Corpus Christi, February 28, 2000

Presenter, Gospel Fest, African American Culture Society, Texas A&M University--Corpus Christi, February 25, 2000

Professional Development Activities

Civil Rights Pilgrimage through Southern Methodist University, March 2010

Strength Quest Workshop, Conference Day, North Lake College, February 2008

Workforce Summit, Globalization and STEM (Science, Technology, Engineering, and Math), February 2008

Introduction to Conflict Dynamics, Continuing Education Course, North Lake College, Spring 2008

Soft Chalk and Blackboard Workshops, North Lake College, Fall 2007

Fulbright Senegal Seminar Workshops, Spring 2006

New Faculty Retreat, Dallas County Community College System, January 2005

Formation Retreat, Dallas County Community College System, Spring 2005

Conference of the College Consortium for International Studies. Washington, DC, March 3-5, 2005

LENS Module Workshop, Dallas County Community College System, 2005

Visions of Excellence, Dallas County Community College System, 2004-2006

College Composition and Communication Conference, San Antonio, TX, March 2004

Reviewer, <u>Alternating Currents</u> by Carol Lea Clark, Houghton Mifflin Publishers, October 2001

Using Quick Access Online—A Writer's Reference, Cedar Valley College, August 30, 2003

Contemporary Ethical Issues in HealthCare, Driscoll Children's Hospital, August 1, 2002

Society of Technical Communication, Region 5 Conference, Houston, Texas, October 13, 2001

Seamless Pipeline Project, Del Mar College, Texas A&M University-Corpus Christi, and Texas A&M University—Kingsville on the Texas A&M University-Corpus Christi Campus, September 13, 2001

WebCT Workshop, Texas A&M University—Corpus Christ, July 6 and 7, 2001

Lilly Conference on College and University Teaching, Southwest Texas State University, August 2-3, 2001

Southwest Texas State University 3rd Annual ExCET Conference, January 13, 2001

Your Syllabus on the Web, CTE Technology Workshop, Texas A&M University—Corpus Christi, January 12, 2001

Texas A&M University System Institute for School-University Partnerships—Academy Conference, Austin, TX, October 2000

Grant Writing Workshop, Del Mar College, September 2000

Summer Teaching Institute, Core Curriculum, Texas A&M University—Corpus Christi, August 2000

Chancellor's Initiative Conference, Texas A&M University System Institute for School-University Partnerships—Houston, TX, June 8-10, 2000

Designing and Evaluating Writing Assignments in the Disciplines, 19th Annual Wildacres' Retreat, Sponsored by University Writing Programs, with the Blumenthal Foundation, Charlotte, NC, May 15-18, 2000

ExCET Changes, SBEC Workshop, Austin, TX, April 2000

Small Business Development, Technical Writing Program Development, Small Business Development Center, Del Mar College, February 4, 2000

Board Member, Board of Supporting Trustees of South Texas Institute for the Arts, Corpus Christi, Texas, 2000

Judge, Decathlon Interview Competition, Corpus Christi Independent School District, January 28, 2000

Decathlon Interview Training, Corpus Christi Independent School District, January 7, 2000

Summer Teaching Institute, Core Curriculum, Texas A&M University— Corpus Christi, August 1999

Using Performance-based Assessment in Your Course, Center for Teaching, Learning & Technology, Bowling Green State University, February 25, 1999

Performance Counseling, The BGSU Training Center, Continuing Education, Bowling Green State University, February 5, 1999

Using Templates to Create Class Web Pages in Claris Home Page, Center for Teaching, Learning & Technology, Bowling Green State University, January 29, 1999

Conflict Management, The BGSU Training Center, Continuing Education, Bowling Green State University, January 22, 1999

Using Chat and Bulletin Board Tools Online—WebCT, Center for Teaching, Learning & Technology, January 22, 1999

WebCT Overview, Center for Teaching, Learning, & Technology, Bowling Green State University, January 11, 1999

Observer, Effective Written Communication, Marathon Oil Company, Hosted by Bowling Green State University Training Center, November 1998

Communicating Across the Full Spectrum: Applications of MBTI, Keirsey Temperament Model, and True Colors, Hosted by the American Society for Training and Development, Toledo Chapter, November 1998

A Model of Hope and Caring: Building Community for African American Women at BGSU, Bowling Green State University, April 1998

Working on the Web, BGSU STC Region 4 Student STC Conference, Bowling Green State University, April 1997

Computers and Writing Conference, El Paso, TX, May 1995

Conference Presentations

Community Colleges for International Development, Inc.: An Association for Global Education 31st Annual Conference, San Antonio, Texas Feb. 19-21, 2007
- "The Senegal, West Africa Fulbright Seminar: Lessons Learned From the Land of Teranga"

School--University Partnerships Conference, San Antonio, Texas October 7-9, 2001
- "The Summer Writing Experience: An Opportunity to Examine and Improve Across-level English/language Arts Classrooms"

Education Service Center, Region 2 Advanced Placement Summer Institute, Corpus Christi, Texas, July13, 2001

"Re-envisioning the Research Paper: An Ethnography Perspective"

Center for Professional Development of Teachers (CPDT) Annual Partnership Conference Corpus Christi, Texas, February 5, 2001.
- "Promoting Family Involvement with Student's Work through School—University Partnership"

National Conference of Teachers of English, Milwaukee, Wisconsin, November 2000
- "Making the Contact in the 'Field': Writing Teachers and Students as Co-Ethnographic Researchers"

Council of Writing Program Administrators, WPA 2000 Conference, Charlotte, North Carolina, July 2000.
- Roundtable: "When Everything is New, What Does 'Change' Mean and How Does It Happen?"

Computers and Writing Conference, Fort Worth, TX, May 2000
- "Advanced Composition, WAC, and Technology: Building Technology Responsible Ties"

Southwest Texas Popular Culture and American Studies, Albuquerque, New Mexico, February 2000
- "Spirituality and Technology: Where's the Education Headed?"

Conference on College Composition and Communication, Atlanta, GA, March 1999
- "Professional Development, My Career or the Program's Image: Whose Community is It?"

National Conference of Teachers of English, Nashville, TN, November 1998
- Roundtable Discussion: New Wine for Old Bottles "Teachers and Students as Co-Learners"
- Recorder/Reactor "The Public Debate about Literacy: What We Know and What We Do"

Teaching, Learning & Technology Roundtables, AAHE and the Ohio College Association, Columbus, OH, October 1998.
- Roundtable Discussion Participant

National Conference of Teachers of English, Detroit, MI, November 1997
- "Building Relationships in Technology and Education: A School/College Collaboration"

National Black Graduate Student Conference, Claremont, CA, May 1996
- "Making Connections: Bridging the Gap between the African American Community and the Academy"

Graduate Student Conference, Texas Tech University, Lubbock, TX, April 1996
- "The Center of A Wheel: Examining the life of Sula"

National Association of African American and Latino Studies, Houston, TX, February 1996
- "A Black Woman's Perspective of Sula"

Appendix B: Preparation for Living the Vision

Women of the Bible I Need to Study in Greater Depth

Godly Traits I Need to Exhibit in My Daily Walk

Supportive Scriptures I'll Meditate On

Supportive Training I'll Explore

Academic Classes I Might Pursue

Volunteer Opportunities I'll Explore

Reading Topics I'll Investigate

Memberships of Helpful Groups I Might Join

Collaborating Partners Who May be Helpful

Mentors Who Could be Supportive

Networking Opportunities I'll Explore

Appendix C: Biblical Women Who Exhibit *REACH* Qualities

Abigail
I Samuel 25:1-42

While her most intimate companion acts foolishly and selfishly, Abigail acts with wisdom and graciousness. She has not become contaminated by her surroundings.

Esther
Esther 3:1- 4: 17

While the entire book of Esther is worth reading, the selected verses illustrate a woman who chose a selfless path in order to intervene on behalf of a persecuted people.

Hannah
I Samuel 1:20

Hannah does not respond to the harshness of one who was close. Rather, she pours her heart out to God to honor her desire.

Lydia
Acts16:11-40

Immediately, we see that Lydia worships; she has a heart for God's Word. As Paul teaches, she listens carefully. She accepts the Lord's guidance in this area. One translation notes that she listens "eagerly." Finally, Lydia's gift of hospitality provides a place for Paul to return after his imprisonment; she serves fellow believers.

Mary the Mother of Jesus
Luke 1:26-38

When the unimaginable is presented to Mary, she responds ultimately with "Here I am . . ." Mary is willing to surrender to the call made on her life, although all the details and forthcoming events are vague.

Tabitha
Acts 9:36-42

Tabitha reveals a labor of love. One translation uses the word "devotion" to illustrate the passion that guides her efforts. Tabitha's contribution to the lives of others so moves people that they share her life's testimony with Peter. Peter is so moved by what he hears that he performs a miracle.

The Woman with an Issue of Blood
Luke 8:40-48

The Woman with an Issue of Blood does not give up; she is relentless, getting to Jesus in spite of the crowd. Furthermore, she exhibits a faith so great that power is put in motion, and Jesus brings attention to the strength of her faith. This woman finally recognizes the ultimate source that can bring health.

The Proverbs 31 Woman
Proverbs 31:10-31

The Proverbs Woman illustrates her full potential in all arenas of her life. There appears to be no strain, no neglect, no chaos, but rather order, forethought, and a prevailing wisdom.

Ruth
Ruth 1:16-17

In the noted verses, Ruth is steadfast and determined. She is compelled by commitment.